*A little t*

# Northar

GW01090522

Personal memories inspired by The Francis Frith Collection®

## THE FRANCIS FRITH COLLECTION

www.francisfrith.com

Based on a book first published in the United Kingdom in 2013 by The Francis Frith Collection®

This edition published exclusively for Bradwell Books in 2013
For trade enquiries see: www.bradwellbooks.com or tel: 0800 834 920
ISBN 978-1-84589-729-1

British Library Cataloguing in Publication Data

A Little Book of Northamptonshire Memories
Personal Memories inspired by the Francis Frith Collection

The Francis Frith Collection
6 Oakley Business Park,
Wylye Road, Dinton,
Wiltshire SP3 5EU
Tel: +44 (0) 1722 716 376
Email: info@francisfrith.co.uk
**www.francisfrith.com**

Printed and bound in Malaysia
Contains material sourced from responsibly managed forests

Front Cover: Thrapston, High Street 1951 T104008p
Frontispiece: Kettering, The Children's Boating Lake, Wicksteed Park c1955  K13001

*The colour-tinting is for illustrative purposes only, and is not intended to be historically accurate*

AS WITH ANY HISTORICAL DATABASE, THE FRANCIS FRITH ARCHIVE IS CONSTANTLY BEING
CORRECTED AND IMPROVED, AND THE PUBLISHERS WOULD WELCOME INFORMATION ON
OMISSIONS OR INACCURACIES

# A little book of Memories – A Dedication

This book has been compiled from a selection of the thousands of personal memories added by visitors to the Frith website and could not have happened without these contributions. We are very grateful to everyone who has taken the time to share their memories in this way. This book is dedicated to everyone who has taken the time to participate in the Frith Memories project.

It is comforting to find so many stories full of human warmth which bring back happy memories of "the good old days". We hope that everyone reading this book will find stories that amuse and fascinate whilst at the same time be reminded of why we feel affection for Britain and what makes us all British.

Francis Frith always expressed the wish that his photographs be made available to as wide an audience as possible and so it is particularly pleasing to me that by creating the Frith web site we have been able to make this nationally important photographic record of Britain available to a worldwide audience. Now, by providing the Share Your Memories feature on the website we are delighted to provide an opportunity for members of the public to record their own stories and to see them published (both on the website and in this book), ensuring that they are shared and not lost or forgotten.

We hope that you too will be motivated to visit our website and add your own memories to this growing treasure trove – helping us to make it an even more comprehensive record of the changes that have taken place in Britain in the last 100 years and a resource that will be valued by generations to come.

John M Buck
Managing Director
www.francisfrith.com

# Pelted with pennies at the Lyric

The Bedford O Type lorry in this photograph of Wellingborough belonged to A J Mackaness Ltd, a local firm, and is delivering fruit and veg. On the right is the old Cosy Café which I remember did a great toasted tea cake and cup of tea. Lower down the street was the Lyric Cinema. On Saturdays they held a children's cinema club matinée (kids from Wellingborough wore the ABC club badge), which featured a live local group as well as the film, serial and cartoons. It was a fiasco playing to these kids (I should know – I did it!), one got pelted with sweets and pennies, and for anyone who can't remember our old currency, pennies were large and heavy....and hurt! Above the cinema was a club called the Lynton Hall Palais, where live music was the order of the day. The Lyric along with the Lynton Hall Palais were reduced to rubble in the 1970s to make way for the Arndale Centre (now known as The Swangate). We lost so much of Wellingborough's character when so many of its old buildings went.

*Mick Austin*

Wellingborough, Midland Road 1949  W279024

# No waiting today!

Wellingborough, Midland Road c1950  W279025

This is a nostalgic picture for drivers of a certain age. The round 'No Waiting' road signs seen on the right hand side of the road in this photograph of Midland Road in Wellingborough is a reminder of when and where you could park your car when you went shopping in the past. These signs were used during the 'unilateral waiting' period in the 1950s, when vehicles could wait on one side of the road on odd days of the month and on the opposite side on even days. The signs were hinged in half moons so that they could be tipped over to show which side of the road was currently available for parking.

*Julia Skinner*

## How our milk was delivered at Welton

My mother's uncles (or possibly older cousins), Tom and Bill Harrison, ran the blacksmiths' on the village green at Welton, just north of Daventry, and they also delivered milk from Church Farm. The milk came up the hill in a churn on a handcart and was ladled into billy cans hanging on the railings of the White Horse pub, whose sign can be seen in the centre of this photograph. As a child in the 1950s it was my job to hang out and collect our billy can.

*James Sherman*

> "The milk came up the hill in a churn on a handcart and was ladled into billy cans."

Welton, High Street c1955  W477010a

# Life in Wellingborough after the war

My family moved to live at 121 Midland Road in Wellingborough during the winter of 1946-47. My father worked in a local paint factory and we children used to collect conkers from the park near our house and give them to our dad for his work, as they needed them to extract the oil for their paint. Our milk was delivered on a horse and cart and poured into jugs at the front door. We kept it in the pantry during the winter and scalded it in the summer, which gave a thick creamy crust for our cornflakes. Bread, meat and fish were also delivered to the door in those days. Our neighbours kept a pig in the back garden near their tennis court, and we used to scratch its back and talk to it. Then one day the pig disappeared and our neighbours' kitchen was full of pork joints! We even tasted some of the bacon – a treat during that time of severe food rationing that continued for some time after the Second World War ended.          *Angela Diamond*

## Feeding the milkman's horse

I lived at Wellingborough from 1959 to 1965, and I remember the horse-drawn milk wagon coming round. I was about 5 or 6 at the time but whenever I heard the clickity-clack of the horse's hooves coming along the road towards our house, 9 The Drive, I would run and get some bread from my mother's cupboard and go to the curb to meet him. The milkman used to let me feed his horse while he delivered our milk. I would walk with them all the way down the road to my friend Alan Dear's house, and then run back home. He was a big white horse as I can remember.
                                                                              *Anthony Wynn*

# Life at Higham Ferrers

My family lived on the Market Square at Higham Ferrers for many years from 1946. My father was the local GP, so we had a car, and later we had a caravan which we used for holidays. In those days caravans were rare and people used to wave to us as we went by! It was a lovely place to grow up in and we played outside all day, weather permitting. After breakfast we'd either put on our roller skates or get on our bikes and spend all day playing in the streets and the Market Square with friends. People were not so over-protective of children in those days and there was not so much traffic! I remember being sent to Battersby's, the grocer at the end of the Market Square, and, having got there, I had usually forgotten what I had been sent to buy! I was too shy to own up so I used to buy something else. I also remember buying sweets and ice-cream from Pashler's. Since it was just after the Second World War, and rationing was in full swing, we could only buy a quarter of sweets, which came out of big jars.

*Susan Barnes*

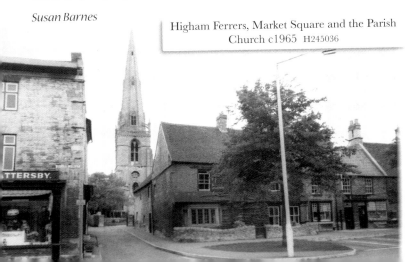

Higham Ferrers, Market Square and the Parish Church c1965   H245036

## Morris overhaul

The Morris car depicted in this photograph was overhauled
and bodied by my late father, Arthur Parker, in 1951-52. He had
removed the body from a c1937 Morris 8 van, overhauled the
mechanics and the chassis, and built from scratch a new
shooting brake-style body. As a 7-year old I was thrilled to be
able to help with the work and immensely proud of the result.
Unfortunately, when my father came to register the car the
authorities decided to demand the full purchase tax which
hadn't been levied on the original pre-war commercial vehicle.
This sum was hard to find in the hard times of the early 1950s,
and the Morris sadly had to be sold to cover it.

*Mr C Parker*

Duston, The Squirrels Inn c1955   D202012

## The Hall at Raunds

I visited The Hall at Raunds regularly as a child in the 1950s and 60s. The library was open there on Mondays and Thursdays and for many years I visited on both days as I was an insatiable reader. You began with one ticket but eventually managed to persuade the librarian to give you two. On Mondays, you were supposed to have one fiction and one non fiction book, but the librarian on Thursdays was much nicer and let you have two story books. The optician was also there on Thursdays so from the age of ten I visited him once a year. The Hall Grounds were wonderful in those days, what a pity so much has been built on. We'd go there on summer Sunday evenings to listen to the Town Band and in some summers a United Charities fete was held there where as Brownies we used to sell crisps and fizzy drinks, 'spruce' we called it. There were side-shows and games, fancy dress parades and one year even a proper fairground roundabout. The fete eventually moved up to the field at the top of Windmill Avenue, but this lacked the charm of the flower-filled gardens of the Hall.

*Wendy Nicolle*

Raunds, The Hall c1955  R82019

# E Coles, Ladies' Outfitter, 37 Brook Street, Raunds

The house on the left of this photograph is where I was born. My mother had the premises built in 1933-34. It had her ladies outfitter's shop underneath (her name, E Coles, can be seen on the board above the shop window), and a living/dining area on the ground floor and bedrooms and a bathroom and living room upstairs. The living room provided an excellent vantage point to view the proceedings at the Methodist Chapel opposite. Never a wedding was missed and my mother would lower the shop blinds when a funeral was in progress. My mother was assisted in the shop by her sister, Hilda Coles, who was responsible for buying at the London fashion houses. Dresses and coats were bought for the shop with the customer in mind and certainly no two ladies in Raunds in those days had the same dress! I remember that in the 1950s nylon stockings were strictly 'under the counter' and for sale to regular customers only! We lived there until moving to Primrose Hill in Raunds in 1958, and the shop eventually closed in 1971.

*Marian Jenny*

Raunds, Brook Street c1960  R82025

# Wellingborough Zoo was one of my favourite places

Wellingborough's zoo opened in 1943 in Croyland Gardens and was a great success in its heyday. The zoo closed around 1970 and the grounds reverted to parkland or were built over with office blocks. A commemorative plaque about the opening of the zoo can be seen on the gate piers of its former entrance from Sheep Street.

My family lived in Wellingborough from 1959 to 1965, and the zoo was one of my favourite places to go as a youngster. I remember how my mother and siblings would scream in delight as we strolled through the zoo viewing the collection of animals, including the wonderful penguins and the beautiful white swans at Swanspool Gardens.

*Anthony Wynn*

The penguin pool from Wellingborough Zoo seen in this view still remains till this very day. It is located in the town centre behind the council offices. If you can cross the brook, it is behind number 7 Doddington Road.

*Jevan Grout*

Wellingborough, The Zoo Park, The Penguins c1950 W279021

## Life at the Old Red Lion at Isham

My grandmother, Mary Jane Abbot, used to run the Old Red Lion pub at Isham and I was born in the room above the old skittle alley in the bar in 1940. I used to help pull pints in the bar, aged 3! My family spent Christmas there most years when I was a child. I remember that the turkey for Christmas dinner was cooked in the ancient baker's oven over the road, the baker used to let many of the villagers use it then.

*Jayne Gilbert*

## And a pint for the lion...

I was interested to read Jayne Gilbert's memory (above) about life at the Old Red Lion pub at Isham on the Frith website. We bought our house at Isham in 1968, which is almost opposite the pub, now (2013) called the Monk & Minstrel. One of the most talked about clients in those days was the lion from Wellingborough Zoo who had once visited the pub and stood with his front paws on the bar while partaking of some liquid refreshment!

*Nigel Stokes*

Isham, Kettering Road and the Old Red Lion pub c1950   I31035

## Childhood memories of Woodford Halse

> Woodford Halse grew from a small ironstone village in the late
> 19th century, partly through ironstone working but mostly when
> the Great Central Railway arrived in 1899. The GCR established a
> station there called Woodford and Hinton, with a four-way railway
> junction, a major locomotive depot and extensive marshalling
> yards. Then in the 1960s the village station and the railway line
> were axed, and a stillness descended on Woodford Halse once more.

My childhood memories of Woodford Halse in the 1950s include
the Hawkes family, whose garden backed on to the Police House
garden. They had one of the first TVs in Woodford – BBC only at
that time of course. Consequently they often had a house full of
children watching it, not to mention a semi-circle of faces outside
the window looking in!

*Ann Fitzgibbon*

My early memories of Woodford Halse in the 1950s include being
taken by bus from Byfield Primary School to the Moravian church
in Parsons Street for the polio injection. Some of my relatives
worked on the railway, and I spent a lot of happy times watching
the comings and goings to the sheds, and watching the 'Master
Cutler' and the 'Yorkshireman', the two high speed mainline trains
at that time.

*Neville Eyles*

I lived in Adams Road in Woodford Halse as a child and my dad and
brother both worked on the railway, I used to stand in our front
garden and listen for them to toot me as they went past. When the
railway was closed down we all started to use the railway bank as a
short cut to school or the shops.

*Vicki Hawkes*

# The train crash at Milton Malsor

On April 18th 1967 I was on a train travelling from Northampton to London. It was a sunny April afternoon, with a few small white clouds drifting across the sky. The train was about a quarter full and we rattled along peacefully until we reached a point just east of Milton Malsor. Suddenly there came the urgent sound of a train's siren blasting repeatedly, followed by violent braking, then the rending of metal and smashing of glass. The train shuddered and vibrated and I got down on the floor, thinking this the safest place. As I crouched there I vividly remember dust particles dancing up and down as we shuddered to a halt, and seeing the pipe of a man who had been smoking near me go bouncing past my nose.

We had collided with an empty coal train travelling north, and many wagons were derailed and flung into a heap. Our front-powered carriage was derailed and pitched down an embankment. After a long stillness and silence we passengers carefully climbed off the train and down the embankment into a field. We did this with some care as the gantries holding the overhead power lines were down and wires were everywhere.

First on the scene was a solitary policeman in a little patrol car but, astonishingly, and this is the point of my story, many ladies carrying a tea urn and cups were next to arrive, and proceeded to sustain us. I understand that they were at a meeting in Milton Malsor (WI?), had seen the crash, and hurried to the scene. British Rail people and ambulances eventually arrived and officialdom took over. Fortunately there were no fatalities, but several people were quite badly injured, including our driver.

I salute the resourceful ladies of Milton Malsor and district for their actions on that day so many years ago!

*David Hills*

## My early days at Byfield, south of Daventry

My childhood memories of Byfield, where I lived on the brand new council estate in Lovett Road in the early 1950s, are idyllic. I was there between the ages of 6 to 10.

We children had to walk what seemed like miles, in all weathers, to the village school which was on the opposite side of the village. Passing the sweet shop on Dolls Hill, where halfpenny chews, sherbet dips and gobstoppers were the treat of the week, we would race down the hill to the stream at the bottom, pass over the bridge, then go through the centre of the old village which had an inn on either side of the road. (One of these, The Rose & Crown, used to be a meeting place for the local Hunt, which was an incredibly exciting and glamorous event. I remember I got 'blooded' one year, much to the horror of my mother.) The smell of fresh bread coming from Mr Smith's bakery used to slow us down, and we used to peer through the door at the very round, pink and flour-covered baker. He had no time for us, so we continued on our way, passing ancient stone houses, some thatched cottages, and high stone walls covered in moss and stonecrop.

The village school must have had only about 50 pupils, if that. It only had two classes when I was there; the elder children were taught by Mr Jackson the headmaster, and we younger ones by 'Miss'. Mr Jackson used to sit on a very high lectern-like wooden desk, so he could see everything that was going on. He terrified me. So did arithmetic, which he taught. In every annual report he commented that 'Rosemarie must learn to overcome her fear of arithmetic'. I never have.

We village children had plenty of activities to keep us entertained. There was the wonderful playing field below the church, where I spent hours on the swings and took many a tumble from the slide onto the gravel. There was no supervision, scabby knees were the norm, and if we hurt ourselves whilst playing we simply cried then started again. My friend John Dunkley and I loved to go to the stream where we used to collect frog spawn and watch the tadpoles develop, catch minnows and sticklebacks, caterpillars, butterflies and ladybirds. I shudder to think how many of these creatures we destroyed in our attempts to understand how their anatomy worked.

I was enrolled into Jean Furburrow's ballet and tap classes in the village. The ballet class was intended to transform me from a tomboy into a young lady, but soon showed I was no budding Margot Fonteyn. Tap dancing was my preference, because I got to wear red shoes and it made a lot of noise. My mother made my tu-tu, as did all the other mums for their daughters, for the big performance we gave at the annual fete on the Vicarage lawn.

Church was a big part of village life. The church was certainly impressive, with a steeple reaching forever, but this was lost on me at the time; more important was playing under the yew trees and a morbid fascination I had for gravestones. Sunday School was obligatory for me but I enjoyed it, though I did play truant one day when the attraction of the nearby playing field was too much of a temptation. I was found out and it never happened again.

I have lived in a tiny rural village in Cyprus for many years now, trying to capture the country life of yesteryear. I have never had the opportunity to revisit Byfield, but it is still very much in my heart.

*Rosemarie Delaney*

*A little book of memories*

## Memories of old Irthlingborough

I'm proud to say I was born and brought up in Irthlingborough (although I don't live there now) and still have fond memories of this lovely old place. From 1956 to 1962 my family lived in part of a large house called The Rookery on the High Street. This adjoined the old Procea Products factory where my father worked for many years as a lorry driver/mechanic. Procea was famous for making slimming bread and it was common to see Procea's lorries parked outside the factory in the High Street, in those days of no yellow lines it wasn't a problem. The Rookery was owned by Procea and split into three houses, we lived in the centre house. Sadly, The Rookery was pulled down in the mid 1960s and a parade of shops was built on its site. The house was grand with large windows and very high ceilings, and today it would have been a listed building and saved for future generations to enjoy.

Irthlingborough, The Cross 1969 133022

Many changes have taken place in Irthlingborough since this photograph of The Cross was taken in 1969, although this part of the town still looks much the same as it did when this view was taken. The market cross was moved to its present location, to the west of its original site, in 1965 to ease the traffic flow – not that I can remember Irthlingborough ever being so popular that it resulted in traffic flow problems, God bless it! The Bull public house to the left of the market cross was the second pub situated on this site. The original Bull was demolished before the war and rebuilt a few feet back from the road in readiness for the widening of the main A6 trunk road to the north, but the effort was wasted as they then decided to by-pass Irthlingborough altogether! The lorry centre right of the picture, in Station Road, belonged to Townsend Carriers from Higham Ferrers and is a BMC-engined Austin delivering parcels. George Burton's paper shop in Station Road (near where the lorry is delivering) is now a pizza parlour – I didn't even know what a pizza was in the 1960s! Nearby was Mr Duncan's chemist shop (famously made of wood), which has now been demolished. Duncan's also sold toys, and how I drooled as a youngster as I looked in his shop window at those wonderful blue and white striped Dinky toy boxes containing every car and lorry in miniature! Mr Duncan always wore a crisp, starched white overall coat, looking every inch a man of the medical world and yet all I ever remember him handing out was pleasure. When we were ill as children it usually meant we'd be given a slug of Lucozade (lovely stuff) from Duncan's. I can still remember the long glass bottle with a screw top and that wonderful transparent amber-coloured wrapper around it. It still amazes me as a feat of advertising and product image that during my childhood Lucozade was meant to aid recovery from illness, yet today it is targeted at fit, athletic people.      *Mick Austin*

# Chopping mangelwurzels at Finedon, near Wellingborough

I wonder how many people remember seeing a field of giant mangelwurzels at Finedon? When I was a lad, Finedon farmers were still following a 15th-century practice of growing the huge white and yellow beetroots for cattle food. I remember seeing several fields of them down Harrowden Lane. As a seven-year old, I had a very intimate acquaintance with them. We lived in Plackett's Yard which abutted the Wallis farm, and I used to go over and 'help' the men working there. One task that gave them great amusement was asking me to get out three mangels for cow feed. Since each mangel was two and a half to three feet long, and weighed about forty pounds, it was quite a task for a little boy. I put my arms around it and wriggled it across the floor to the turnip chopper. The men took a spade and cut the mangel into several pieces which they tossed into the hopper. The chopper had a cylinder with four knives set into it, a handle to turn, and two big flywheels. Once it got going you could toss chunks into the hopper, and a steady stream of tasty chunks for the cattle would come out the bottom. Once in a while the chunks would jam in the hopper. Patience was required then, because you had to wait for the wheels to stop before you re-arranged the chunks. Sometimes people got impatient, reached into the hopper and lost an arm…

*Peter Munton*

> "You could toss chunks into the hopper, and a steady stream of tasty chunks for the cattle would come out the bottom."

# When the Beatles didn't come to Wellingborough!

On 6th November 1963 the Beatles were playing at the ABC cinema in Northampton and word got around that the famous 'Fab Four' were staying at the Hind Hotel in Wellingborough. The place was surrounded by fans hoping to get a closer look at John, Paul, George and Ringo…alas, they were all deprived of this chance, not only were the Beatles not staying at the hotel but they weren't staying at any local hotel! In fact, the Beatles ended their performance in Northampton with 'Twist & Shout' and as the National Anthem was playing in the cinema they made their getaway via a factory in St Michael's Road to be escorted by police back down the M1 to London. Apparently no one in the audience that night heard a note of what they played over the screaming!     *Mick Austin*

Wellingborough, The Hind Hotel and Sheep Street c1955  W279050

*A little book of memories*

## This is where I bought my suits

When this photograph was taken in the mid 1950s, I was in the Merchant Navy. When on leave, I regularly purchased a suit from the Burton tailor's shop, which is just in view to the extreme right. The street has not changed much physically during the past fifty years or so, but some of the old pubs have long disappeared.

*Kenneth Taylor*

Kettering, Silver Street c1955   K13022

# The bakery on Bakehouse Hill

The bakery seen behind the lamp post in this view of Bakehouse Hill at Kettering was a regular visit for us children on Saturday mornings in the late 1940s when we used to go to the morning picture shows at the cinema. We would call in there to buy freshly baked crusty rolls to eat during the film, but they were usually consumed long before we got to our seats!

*Kenneth Taylor*

> "We would call in there to buy freshly baked crusty rolls to eat during the film."

Kettering, Bakehouse Hill c1955  K13044

## Bus station memories

I was catching the 259 bus service from bay 5 of Kettering Bus Station at about the time this photograph was taken, then in 1970 I was working on the buses as a conductor, and by 1974 I was a bus driver. As seen in this photo, the buses were reversed into the bays in the 1960s, this changed in the mid 1970s with the introduction of more front entry buses, from then we drove into the bays and reversed off. At the far end of the bus station was a café and at this end was a waiting room and booking office. A block of flats now stands on this site.
*Derek Fox*

## Running for the bus!

Back in the early 1970s I used to wait in the queue at Kettering's bus station to catch the number 254 bus for Broughton where I used to live. If I just missed the bus, I used to sprint down the hill and up to Northampton Road to catch up with it there, as the bus had to go round the hospital and cemetery before reaching Northampton Road. That was when I was young and fit!                    *Bryan Whalley*

Kettering, The Bus Station c1965  K13079

# Happy memories of an evacuee to Barton Seagrave

During the Second World War I was evacuated from London to Miss Scott's cottage at Barton Seagrave in Northamptonshire, which was sited opposite the village smithy, the one-storey building seen to the right of the lorry in this photograph. I arrived there on 1st September 1939, the day after my 11th birthday. On my first day in Barton I was given a bedroom in the attic that had a small window where I used to watch the smith at work. It was my favourite place to sketch. My sisters were also evacuated to Barton Seagrave, they initially went to the hall and then to Mr and Mrs Henson's on Barton Road. We enjoyed our time living in the village, the kids accepted us, and we roamed the fields and trespassed in the spinney. My best wishes go to all those who made us welcome in those dark days.

*Tom Andrews*

Barton Seagrave, Botolph's Road c1960   B700023

# Childhood memories of Northampton

I was born in Northampton in 1940, and lived there until 1953. The children of my generation were probably the last to have real freedom, able to go unattended to the parks, Saturday morning pictures, and virtually anywhere we wanted to. This did not mean we were feral by any means – in those days, no one was afraid to stop children doing wrong, and you knew that if your dad found out you had caused any trouble, you were in hot water. A highlight of the week for me and my friends was the Saturday morning trip to the 'Temp' or New Coliseum cinemas and what value for money it was, 6d for a cartoon, the Pathé News, an instalment of the latest serial and then the main film. As there was no TV in those days you made your own fun, which meant you joined the Scouts, Boys Brigade, YMCA or the Roadmender's boxing club, and you also went out more as a family. On Saturday nights, my family went to the Twentieth Century Club, where my dad played in a little dance band. It was a regular Saturday night out, and my mum's brothers and sisters used to turn up too for a night of dancing and fun – that was great, as it meant we children had an extra bottle of lemonade and packet of crisps when they turned up. On Sunday night at the club it was the 'turns' which took the stage. The turns were anything from performing dogs to singers. My last memory of the Twentieth Century Club before moving away from Northampton is of my dad playing with the band there, one of three functions he did on the day when Queen Elizabeth II was crowned in 1953. We only went to the function at the club, which was at midday, and then went to a Coronation Day party afterwards and my dad went off to play at the other functions which were elsewhere in the town. Something I remember is that it rained mostly all that day.                    *Sydney Claydon*

My brother and I were evacuated as children from London to Northampton during the Second World War. We lived in Alma Street, me at number 21 with an elderly aunt and uncle, my brother at number 40. Opposite the top end of Alma Street was a church with a school next door which we both attended. As 'London kids' we were always sat at the back of the class, and moved from one class to another. Occasionally milk was handed out in mugs, we had to wait until last and sometimes there was none left so we went without. I remember there were bomb shelters in the playground for us pupils to shelter in if there was an air-raid. On one of the roads near Alma Street was a fish and chip shop, and we struck up a friendship with the lad who lived there. One day when we called for him, his father had just given him some chips and shouted "Don't give them to those bloody London kids". Most of the local kids avoided playing with us, and we spent a lot of time playing by ourselves in the meadows at the bottom end of Alma Street, with a bottle of cold tea as a treat. I have no doubt that many local people treated us well, but we had come from London where, as young as we were, we had become accustomed through the Blitz to helping and supporting each other, and being shut out was something we could not understand. I must say though that our carers who had taken us in did their best under very difficult circumstances to look after us, something we have always respected and appreciated.

When Dad returned from Africa on leave from the Army we persuaded our parents to take us back to London. We spent the rest of the war dodging the 'doodlebugs' (V1 and V2 rockets) and we had some close shaves, but we made it. It's funny how some things stay with you for life, I am now in my seventies and I honestly believe the short time I spent in Northampton made me more tolerant towards others in later life.

*Ron Large*

## My mother's boutique, Calico Casa, in Northampton

The photograph below shows the north side of Northampton's Market Square as it looked around 1950. All the buildings seen here have been demolished, including the grandiose Emporium Arcade of 1901 and the Mercury & Herald offices to its left. The buildings went mainly to make way for the Grosvenor Centre shopping malls.

My mother, Gillian Mayes, ran a boutique in Northampton throughout the 1970s, named Calico Casa. Her first little shop was in the (now demolished) Emporium Arcade off the Market Square, then she moved premises to 29 York Road where she stayed for many years. She sold beautiful hand-made women's and children's garments, including long flowing gypsy skirts and crocheted tops. I wonder how many people remember Calico Casa, and perhaps still have one of her garments tucked away in their wardrobe somewhere!

*Christobel Amelia Hastings*

Northampton, Market Square c1950  N40009

# That's where I bought my wedding outfit!

When I read Christobel Hastings' memory (opposite) about her mother's shop, Calico Casa, on the Frith website, it struck a chord with me. Her mother made my wedding outfit in 1973 from her shop in York Road. She made me a maxi skirt with a waistcoat, and I purchased a floaty blouse to wear with it. In the evening the blouse and waistcoat were removed and I wore the halterneck top she had also made me, to match the maxi. I still have them all somewhere.                     *Helen West*

*One of Northampton's now-lost buildings is seen on the right of this photograph, the old Notre Dame High School which was built in 1871 as a school and convent run by the Sisters of Notre Dame de Namur. A former teacher at the school was believed to haunt the building. The ghost was only seen from the knees up, and it is believed that the floor level of the hall that she walked across had been raised since the teacher's death. The school has now been demolished and replaced with shops and offices.* Julia Skinner

Northampton, Abington Street and Notre Dame High School c1955  N40060

*A little book of memories*

## Great days in the park

I was born in 1951 in Lutterworth Road, Northampton, just a five minutes' walk from one of the most beautiful parks in the country – Abington Park. Originally part of the Wantage family estate, it boasted a museum (formerly the Manor House), a church, three lakes, aviaries, and a bandstand. It was a truly magical place for a young boy in the 1950s. Every summer during the school holidays I would be found with the rest of my Barry Road Primary School gang in the park (apart from when I and my family were on our annual summer holiday to Margate). An average day spent in the park would be something as follows:

After breakfast I'd head for Sid Child's, the newsagents, on the corner of Lutterworth Road to buy my 'ammunition' (three rolls of one penny caps) for my six-shooters and 'rations' (sweets – one lucky bag, four fruit salads, and four black jacks). With my supplies I'd head to the 'Monkey House' in the park to meet the rest of the gang. I never quite found out what the 'Monkey House' was and how it got its name, the Park Café (formerly called Ye Olde Oak Café) stands in its place now. Once all the gang had assembled, we then decided the plan of action for the morning. As we were nearly always armed with an assortment of weaponry, such as Roy Roger's six-shooters, Davy Crockett rifles, Tommy guns and cap bombs, it would be a game of 'Germans and English' – never 'Cowboys and Indians', perhaps because they never had Tommy guns in those days! Then we headed off to the spinney. The spinney was a great place, full of trees and bushes and with a stream running through it, an ideal place for den-building, battles, bird-nesting, and dam-building. Sometimes if we were lucky one of the park's gardeners had had a bonfire and we would rekindle it into a good old blaze.

At lunch time, with all our sweet rations gone, we'd troop off to one of the gang's home, usually my mate Charlie Ward's, as he lived nearest the park; even though we were unannounced, his mum would always muster up some potted beef or bloater paste sarnies and – if we were lucky – a piece of home-made fruit cake, washed down with Tizer or lemonade (tea was for adults only). The afternoons saw us back in the park, usually doing something more leisurely after the morning's strenuous activities. Sometimes it would be crayfish hunting on the big lake, or catching minnows or newts.

Although the summer holidays always seemed hot and sunny in those days, even a sudden downpour didn't dampen our fun. The museum would be the place to head for then. It boasted a great collection of stuffed animals, birds and fish, and there was a case of exotic birds and a case with two swans in, and then there was the Egyptian Room with a real mummy's tomb in it. We'd try to scare each other by walking like a mummy and making ghostie noises, this in turn would attract the museum attendant. He used to follow us from room to room to make sure we didn't misbehave, but we always knew when he was approaching by the sound of his footsteps on the old creaky wooden floorboards. After our visit (and pocket money allowing) we would finish the day having a wafer ice-cream in the café inside the museum or sitting outside in the courtyard.

Abington Park was a very special place to us boys in the late 1950s, not just in the summer holidays but in all seasons. In autumn we went there collecting conkers, chestnuts and bags of leaves to stuff our Guy Fawkeses in readiness for door-door 'Penny-for-the-Guy' collecting (all proceeds being spent on sweets and one penny bangers). Winters too were good fun in the park, when there had been a fall of snow everyone would head to the 'tower' by the boating lake with their home-made sledges. They were great days.              *Andrew Beardsmore*

# The Changing Face of Corby

Corby's development into the large modern town of today took off with the coming of the railway in 1875. The vast ironstone deposits of the area had been exploited in Roman and Anglo-Saxon times, and during the railway's construction in the 19th century they were rediscovered. A Birmingham industrialist, Samuel Lloyd, investigated the possibility of commercial ironstone quarrying and processing and in 1910 he began the commercial production of iron. Lloyd's company amalgamated with a Scottish tube-making firm in 1903 to become Stewarts & Lloyds, and the company went from strength to strength in the following years until 1932, when Corby was chosen to be the site of one of the biggest iron and steel-making complexes in the world. This was the period of Britain's Great Depression, and swarms of newcomers arrived here looking for desperately needed employment, coming mainly from the north of England and Scotland. For some time Corby was known locally as 'Little Scotland' because of the large number of Scottish migrant workers who had come to live and work in the Steel Works there. Thousands of new

Corby, Stewarts & Lloyds Steel Works c1955   C337004

homes and other facilities had to be built, transforming Corby almost overnight from a village into a modern industrial town. In 1950 another milestone in Corby's development took place, with the town being granted New Town status, and many more new buildings and housing developments sprang up in the 1950s and 1960s.

This photograph of the Steel Works in the 1950s shows (from left to right) the four blast furnaces, the Brassert towers (gas cleaners), and the cooling towers. A Barclay saddleback engine can be seen on the right, heading in the direction of the tall floodlight in the foreground. The nationalisation of the iron and steel industry in 1967 led to Stewarts & Lloyds becoming part of the British Steel Corporation, but in 1979 the Government decided to close the Steel Works at Corby, to the great dismay of many local people. Everything seen in this photograph of the Stewarts & Lloyds Steel Works has since been demolished, and much of the surrounding area has been redeveloped as a retail park and industrial estate.

One of the most recognisable of all the buildings of the Steel Works was 'The Corby Candle', a large chimney that burned off gases produced by the steelmaking process which could be seen from many miles away.

## We remember the Corby Candle

The old blast furnaces of the Steel Works used to turn Corby's night sky orange. It never got dark in the Corby of my childhood. The Corby Candle and all the steel and tube mills lit the night up.    *Kenneth Little*

I can remember the Corby Candle, and the flames lighting up the sky when they opened the furnaces at the works.    *Linda Briggs*

# A worrying incident at the air-raid shelter

During the Second World War a large underground air-raid
shelter was built on the roundabout on Studfall Avenue at
Corby, near the Open Hearth pub, but I'm not sure the shelter
was ever used. One day when I was playing on the shelter with
my friends I used a very mild swear word, and was overheard by
a lady who knew my parents and threatened to tell them. She
didn't, but as a ten-year-old I had a pretty worrying day or two!

*Robert Hughes*

# A bizarre wartime experiment at Corby

I wonder if anyone else who lived in Corby during the war
remembers a bizarre experiment which took place in the town
in 1941 or 42. Large containers of diesel, or some sort of oil,
were placed at intervals on the grass verges outside houses, a
short chimney was attached to each one and topped by a disc
with three prongs. At night, members of the Pioneer Corps lit
a plug which caused a black, smelly cloud to roll out of each
container. If the idea was to blank out the blast furnaces at the
Steel Works to make them invisible and protect them from
air-raid attack, it was completely ineffective and the smoke
must have aggravated anyone with chest problems. I lived on
Thoroughsale Road at the time, and I remember it took years
for the verges to recover. There was no Health & Safety then!

*Robert Hughes*

# How Corby helped win the war

This photograph shows the now-demolished Pluto pub at Corby, which used to stand on Gainsborough Road. Its name was a reminder of a significant part played by the former Steel Works at Corby in the war effort during the Second World War. PLUTO was an acronym formed from the initial letters of 'Pipe Line Under The Ocean', the codename for the production of hundreds of miles of steel tubing at Corby which was used for conveying fuel across the English Channel to the Allied Forces in Europe, following the D-Day landings in 1944.

*Julia Skinner*

Corby, The Pluto, Gainsborough Road c1960   C337067

# When I was young in Corby...

In 1957, when I was a baby, I moved with my family into a brand
new Corporation house on the Beanfield estate at Corby, 32 Thirsk
Road. My father had got work in the steelworks at Corby and had
been living at Weldon in Stewarts & Lloyds' accommodation for a
year or so before my mum and myself came down from Scotland.
Judging by the photo of Hazel Leys Secondary Modern School on the
opposite page, Gainsborough Road was yet to be extended to enter
the lower Beanfield estate when this view was taken around 1960.
There was a brook where the photographer was standing, which I
remember was teeming with freshwater life when I was very little.
I used to fish and play there a lot with my friends, then over the
course of my childhood I watched this lovely brook turn into nothing
more than a sewer with nothing able to survive in it, no doubt a
consequence of the urban build-up of the Beanfield and Lincoln
estates. When I was small I used to go for walks with my mum and
little sister in the fields to the right of this photo, which became the
Lincoln and Kingswood estates. Ponies were tethered in these fields
and the one at the top towards the woods was cow pasture, where
I once saw a deer grazing. This all changed in the 1960s when the
Lincoln estate was built. During its construction the whole area was
a massive playground for us kids, there were no barriers or walls in
those days to keep people out of building sites. We had a ball playing
in the construction site at weekends and early evenings when the
workmen had packed up and gone home. I attended Hazel Leys
Secondary Modern School between 1968 and 1972. Most of the green
space seen in this photo of the school was made into playing and
sports fields for the schools, though a line of trees, one of which I
helped to plant, was in place by the end of the 1960s.      *Kenneth Little*

# Short skirts and sateen knickers at Hazel Leys Secondary Modern School at Corby

What memories the photos and comments on the Frith website about Corby in the 1950s and 60s brought back to me, especially about Hazel Leys Secondary Modern School, which I attended at that time. I particularly remember Miss Humphries, who used to measure our skirts to ensure they were regulation length. I'm sorry to say that due to her eagle eye I was pulled up a few times for failing this, and subsequently had to unroll the waistband of my skirt to lower my skirt until she was satisfied. I also remember hiding down by the brook with a couple of like-minded souls when we had cross country running which we hated, then getting caught and having to complete the course and also being given detention. Oh, those days of black sateen gym knickers – so very flattering!

*Glynis Young*

Corby, Hazel Leys Secondary Modern School c1960  C337068

## Shopping at Pearks

I lived in Corby in the 1950s, when I was young. I remember going to get groceries from Pearks Stores in Occupation Road. It had those green and white (or black) mosaic tiles on the walls, and old fashioned scales. I recall that I loved the Spam they sold! All the staff wore immaculate white overalls and hats.

*Polly Short*

## Whizzing canisters and broken biscuits

*I lived with my family in Burns Drive at Corby in the 1950s. I can remember walking down to the Studfall Avenue shops and also some of the shops in 'old' Corby. I particularly remember an ironmonger's with one of those old-fashioned systems for sending the cash whizzing along to the cash desk in little canisters! I also recall a grocer's shop with big tins of broken biscuits that were sold cheap!*

Linda Briggs

## I had never seen an old person before!

Corby was a very young place in 1965, not just the New Town but its people as well. The expanding steelworks attracted thousands of young migrants, mainly from Scotland. I recall an occasion when I was about four on a bus with my mum travelling to Kettering, the nearest town to Corby. This very strange woman got on the bus who had lines and wrinkles all over her face. I stared and stared at her until my mum told me off for being rude. The woman smiled at us then she said, in what I was to come to recognise as the local Northamptonshire accent, that I was to be forgiven. She remarked that I probably had never seen an old person before. She was right. It seems strange now, but everybody in Corby at that time was young, including the adults.

*Kenneth Little*

# Long-ago days in Corby

My family came to Corby in 1956 from Staffordshire. My dad, Ted Simmons, was the groundsman for the Stewarts & Lloyds Recreation Club (Welfare Institute) in Occupation Road and we lived on Thoroughsale Road (which was hard to spell when you were small). I remember going to the Studfall shops when we first got to Corby and I couldn't understand anyone because they all had Scottish accents. I remember going to the children's Saturday morning club, playing in Thoroughsale Woods, which I thought were huge, and dances at the 'Bin'. Even though Corby was fairly big we kids were allowed to walk everywhere by ourselves. I thought the town centre was large and that's when it ended at Woolworth's, and I loved the market. My school uniforms were bought at the Co-op in the town centre. I attended the Samuel Lloyd School for Girls, and me and my friends used to spend our school dinner money in the Tipaldi's café in Rockingham Road. Then I went to Corby Tech and thought myself very grown up. Those days seem a long time ago now.

*Joan Simmons*

Corby, Corporation Street 1960 C337042

## Memories of Corby market

I have childhood memories of getting off the number 32 bus at Corby's original bus station and running into the market. I always had urgent business in those days that demanded maximum haste, such as getting to Woolworth's to buy an Airfix model. The market was always busy. I remember one stall that sold American comic books. They were always popular with us kids. For sixpence you could buy the latest Bat Man or Spider Man edition. The stories were great but best of all was the sheer Americanism of the comics, with their zip codes and prices in cents.

*Kenneth Little*

I lived in Corby from 1960 to 1979. I remember a man named Geoff who sold fabric on the market. His 'tape measure' for measuring one yard of fabric was the length from his nose to the end of his fingers, so you always had enough for a dress and some left over – he could never measure a yard right and always gave too much!

*Lily Redmond*

Corby, Market Square c1965   C337164

*Northamptonshire*

# Saturday morning pictures at the Odeon in Corby

Saturday morning could not come quick enough for me and my brother Marty, when we'd walk 5 miles from our home to the morning picture show at the Odeon cinema in Rockingham Road in Corby. We'd be excitedly looking forward to cartoons with Mickey Mouse, and on-going serials with the Lone Ranger or Flash Gordon where the end finished with the hero about to come to a nasty end, so you had to come back next week to see what happened. The shows usually started with a sing-song generated by a compère, then a game show, different each week, like eating a doughnut on a string the fastest or, my favourite, a singing contest. The first one I won was singing 'She Loves You' by the Beatles. I won a big bag of mixed sweets that me and my brother shared with all our mates. I remember in the tough winter of 1963 we walked to the cinema up to our knees in snow to get there and were most annoyed to find it could not open. I remember thinking "Well, I walked 5 miles, what's the problem!". That's how much we enjoyed our films.    *John O'Connor*

My sister Linda and I also went to the Odeon at Corby on a Saturday morning for the children's cinema club. We used to sing a song:

*'We come along on Saturday morning, greeting everybody with a smile.*
*We come along on Saturday morning, knowing it's all worthwhile.*
*We're members of the Odeon and all intend to be*
*Good citizens when we grow up and emperors of the sea.*
*We come along on Saturday morning, greeting everybody with a smile, smile,*
*Greeting everybody with a smile.'*

Jeanette Laufer (née Simpson)

# Daventry Rec Steam Engine

This old steam engine spent its working life in Byfield stone quarry until it closed in 1965, and was then moved to the recreation ground at Daventry where it became a great attraction for the local children. It has now been removed from the recreation ground, largely because of Health & Safety considerations.

Daventry, The Recreation Ground c1965   D83085

## Our favourite old chuffer

It was lovely to see this great photo of the recreation ground at Daventry on the Frith website. This was my local 'rec' and I played here every day without fail. I remember the engine being installed and playing on it long before the Health & Safety guys realised its dangerous potential. We found everything worked – the boiler door opened, and you could crawl inside to hide. All the levers worked and it was probably after some poor kid lost a finger or got stuck inside the boiler that the authorities made it 'safe'! It really was a fantastic addition to the 'rec' and we played in it, on it and around it constantly.

*Martin Ellacott*

## No-one ever found me!

*I remember the day in the mid 1960s that this steam engine arrived in the recreation ground at Daventry. It was a source of great entertainment for us youngsters, particularly as originally everything was accessible. I remember climbing up on the footplate and seeing a little lad emerging from the firebox. It was rumoured that it was possible to get into the boiler and exit up the funnel but I never saw that done! It was great for playing hide and seek – I found one hiding place that no-one ever found. Sadly, even back then, steel plates were soon welded over the more interesting points of access but it remained a popular attraction on every visit to the 'rec'. One proof of male bravado amongst the 9 to 12-year-olds was jumping off the roof of the engine onto the grass below.* Dave Cairns

## Running through the graveyard

I regularly took a short cut through the graveyard of Holy Cross
Church at Daventry (below) when I was a kid in the 1960s and early
1970s. If it was dark or foggy it was very, very spooky and I used to run
like hell – I was a good runner!

*Martin Ellacott*

## Picking up the signal through the toaster

In 1925 the BBC chose Borough Hill near Daventry as the site for
their new national radio transmitter, which would bring a 'National'
service to everyone in Britain from one site. This was followed in
1932 by the opening of the Empire Station. The masts and aerials
on Borough Hill were a feature of the landscape for over 65 years,
and Daventry continued to broadcast to the world until 1992, when
the facility was transferred to other BBC World Service sites. Many
Daventry people reminisce about hearing the General Overseas
Service's signature tune, 'Lillibulero', being picked up and transmitted
through their electric kettles and toasters!

*Julia Skinner*

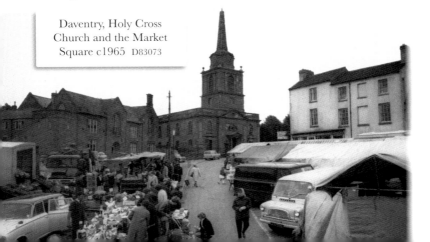

Daventry, Holy Cross
Church and the Market
Square c1965  D83073

# Childhood memories of Oundle

My family lived in Peter Street in Oundle when I was a young child. Our house was on the right side going down the hill, which is where I first learned to ride a bike in 1970, my elder sister giving me a push at the top of the hill... stopping was the problem! Across the road were open fields where we would fossick for Roman pottery shards with our father, and at the top of the street there was a conker tree which entertained my friends and I for hours.

*Richard Harvey*

> "I first learned to ride a bike in 1970, my elder sister giving me a push at the top of the hill... stopping was the problem!"

Oundle, New Street c1950 O103029

## A Royal Love Story

When I used to visit my grandmother at Geddington I always loved to hear her tell the sad but romantic story about the old medieval monument in the village centre, seen here in this quaint 1920's view. It is one of the twelve 'Eleanor Crosses' built to commemorate Eleanor of Castile, the beloved wife of Edward I who died in 1290 whilst she and the king were at Harby in Nottinghamshire. Her body was taken from there to London for burial in Westminster Abbey, and the king later had a series of commemorative crosses built at the places along the route where her funeral cortege rested for the night. Only three of the original crosses remain – the other two are at Hardingstone, also in Northamptonshire, near Northampton (although damaged, it remains a landmark on the London road), and Waltham Cross in Hertfordshire – and Geddington's is the best preserved. The monument contains a number of small statues of the queen (who was probably 13 when she married Edward, and bore him a total of 16 children), and stands as a sad commemoration of a royal love story.

*Julia Skinner*

Geddington, The Village 1922  72253

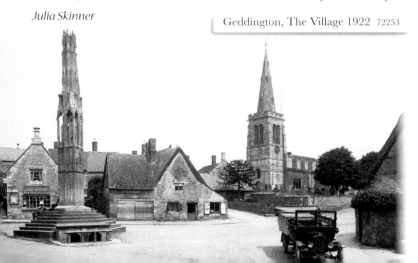

# The best years of my life

I have happy memories indeed of growing up in Earls Barton, near Wellingborough. For an eight-year-old living in the village in the mid 1950s it was heaven. I remember long summer evenings and school holidays playing in woods, open fields and on building sites, or cycling (yes, at eight) to Overstone Park or down to Castle Ashby station to watch the trains from Northampton and Wellingborough come past. Memories of the smell of leather from the shoe factory on North Street come flooding back to me, along with memories of Lyons Maid ice-creams and Jublies from Ingram's shop on Victoria Street. I also remember the village 'bobby', who was called Mr Bosworth. He once gave me four lashes of the strap and confiscated my bike for four days just because I nicked a few First World War rifles that I found in an annexe next to the church. I tried to sell them for sixpence each to my mates.

When I went to the primary school at Earls Barton in the mid 1950s it was run by a headmaster called Mr Goodbody, assisted by the arch dragons Miss Elson and Miss Clark. They were terrible teachers but good at banging books on your head from behind if they thought you weren't paying attention – the fact that you may have been was totally irrelevant. Every lunch time I walked from school to my home on Elizabeth Way in the village and I remember how quiet the roads were, with hardly any cars about in those days. I wonder who else from that time recalls the siren that used to go off at exactly 1 o'clock? I had to be at the bottom of Manor Road when it started otherwise I was late back at school. However, in spite of the liberally applied strap or books banged on my head at school, those really were the happiest days of my life and although I moved from the village in 1958 my affection for it remains.

*Peter Dixon*

## Lovely Mrs Bishop of Boddington School

I attended the village school at Upper Boddington (south-west of
Daventry) from 1946-1951. My teacher at first was Miss Semper, who
I do not remember too well. After her came Mrs Pat Bishop who
was a lovely lady, she and her husband lived in the school house
in the playground. She was influential in getting the first children
from Boddington through to Grammar School, giving them extra
classes after school in her own home. I also remember her getting
us musical instruments, and taking us down the fields to study
wildlife and flowers. She had a dog which had too many puppies
to feed, and we used to bottle feed some of the pups after school.
Mrs Bishop was a wonderful teacher, and influenced all our lives, I
am sure. There were still only about 2 dozen children at the school
when I left, I believe the village had approximately 100 residents in
those days, as did Lower Boddington.           *Maureen Tuffin (Simpson)*

## My childhood memories of Byfield

*My family lived in Byfield when I was young in the 1950s, next door to the
village primary school. In those days Byfield had three grocers, two butchers,
a bakery, a drapery, two sweet shops, a bicycle repair shop, a radio repair shop,
a general clothing/toy/knitting wool shop, four pubs, a garage, a church and
three chapels. There were only about 700 people in the village then, but our
needs were well met. Byfield School still looks the same as it did when I was
a pupil there. In those days it was girls and infants in the back playground,
boys in the front. There were three classes; the Infants had an open fire,
Lower Junior room was stepped, and the Upper Juniors had the technology
for School's Wireless. We listened to 'Singing Together', 'Rhythm and Melody',
'People, Places and Things'. It was as exciting as web access today.* Penny Lucas

## How I spent my school holidays

*In our school summer holidays in the 1970s I used to go fishing and swimming down the brook below where I lived, at number 19 Pioneer Avenue in Desborough. Me and my friends also roamed the allotments and surrounding fields, armed with catapults and pockets full of stones. Towards the end of the holidays the allotments were full of trees laden with fruit just calling out to us to go scrumping, trying not to get caught or seen by the allotment owner. If that happened, the words I used to dread hearing would ring out: "Young Oram, I know it's you, wait till I see your dad!" All good harmless fun until you got home to a clip around the ear.*

Sean Oram

## One door for boys and the other for girls

I did 3 years at the Church Junior School at Brackley (below), which was an old type of school with one door for boys and the other for girls. The heating was from coke-burning boilers and we had to go across the playground to the outside toilets. Lovely in winter!

*Ian Haverly*

Brackley, The Church Junior School c1955  B698003

## The A5 Rangers Cycling Club

Does anyone from Towcester remember the A5 Rangers Cycling Club? I was one of the early members of this club. At weekends in the late 1940s groups of us, boys and girls, would cycle all over the county, singing as we went. We usually stopped for tea somewhere, most often at Marsh Gibbon, before making the journey back to Towcester. Our meeting room was a cottage off Watling Street, which was loaned to us by Mr England – both he and his daughter Mavis were keen members of the club. My cycling days are well behind me now, but old members of the club may remember me as 'Snowy'.

*Doug McKeown*

Towcester, Watling Street c1955   T105007

## The Shops in Church Street

When I lived in Lower Weedon in the 1950s, my parents had a shop at the end of Church Street, which was our family home until Dad decided to retire to Badby. Further up the street was the cobbler's shop and Mr Gate's coal merchants. Can you imagine, we had four shops all in that one street in the 1950s, most villages are lucky to have one now!

*Diane Barlow*

## Short back and sides please!

Somewhere on the left of this street (below) was a barbershop when I was young. I had my first ever haircut as a boy there, in about 1957

*Alan M*

Thrapston, High Street 1951  T104008

*A little book of memories*

## A few drinks at the Duke...

My memory of the Duke of Wellington pub at Stanwick is that this was the first public house that I ever got drunk in. I was 17 and had just joined up in the Army in Boy Service. It was the Christmas of 1958, I was on leave and on Boxing Day I went with family friends to the Duke. I was told I was not old enough to drink, but my companions said if I was old enough to wear a uniform I was old enough to drink. So they filled me up with Double Diamond beer…

*Trevor Morris*

Stanwick, The Duke of Wellington c1965   s628003

# I was a high tipper here

In 1958 I visited the Blue Bell Inn at Rothwell and spent only a modest amount, however I left half a crown as a tip because of a very nice waitress. I left, and had walked about two blocks when the lady chased me down to thank me. I was quite surprised at this, but managed to remain calm and smiled graciously!

*Jim Haynes*

Rothwell, The Blue Bell Inn c1965   R322055

# Working at Kettering Tyres Ltd at Rushden

I joined Kettering Tyres Ltd in Newton Road in Rushden in the late 1960s, as assistant to the late Cedric 'Tiny' Guilford, who was a larger than life character in every way – he weighed 20-odd stone and had a personality to match. At this time the Labour Minister for Transport, Barbara Castle, had just introduced a new law requiring tyres to have a minimum depth of tread. Our problem then was not selling tyres but being able to get them in the first place, and every morning I would make a detour into work at Rushden from my home in Kettering to the company Head Office in Wellingborough to try and fill my elderly Hillman Husky estate car with whatever tyres were available!

*Adrian Speakman*

Rushden, The War Memorial c1965   R223018

# My grandmother was the head cook at Castle Ashby

In the 1940s and 50s my grandmother, Cecelia (called Cissy) was the head cook at Castle Ashby, one of the seats of the Marquess of Northampton. I got to know many of the staff, and used to play in the gardens of the house. One thing that has always stuck in my memory is of when my grandmother was ill at one stage, and looking out of her bedroom window and seeing the text in the lettering of the balustrades that separate the terraces of the garden, matching the lettering on the parapet of the house. Part of it reads 'The grass withers, the flower fadeth, but the word of our God lasteth for ever', and because of this it has always been one of my favourite Bible verses. I shall always be grateful to Lady Northampton because she paid for me as a 7-year-old to have a surgeon to come over to this country to perform a unique heart operation on me which was not available in this country.

*Jane Folkes*

Castle Ashby 1922   72221

# FRANCIS FRITH

## PIONEER   VICTORIAN   PHOTOGRAPHER

Francis Frith, founder of the world-famous photographic archive, was a complex and multi-talented man. A devout Quaker and a highly successful Victorian businessman, he was philosophical by nature and pioneering in outlook. By 1855 he had already established a wholesale grocery business in Liverpool, and sold it for the astonishing sum of £200,000, which is the equivalent today of over £15,000,000. Now in his thirties, and captivated by the new science of photography, Frith set out on a series of pioneering journeys up the Nile and to the Near East.

## INTRIGUE AND EXPLORATION

He was the first photographer to venture beyond the sixth cataract of the Nile. Africa was still the mysterious 'Dark Continent', and Stanley and Livingstone's historic meeting was a decade into the future. The conditions for picture taking confound belief. He laboured for hours in his wicker dark-room in the sweltering heat of the desert, while the volatile chemicals fizzed dangerously in their trays. Back in London he exhibited his photographs and was 'rapturously cheered' by members of the Royal Society. His reputation as a photographer was made overnight.

## VENTURE OF A LIFE-TIME

By the 1870s the railways had threaded their way across the country, and Bank Holidays and half-day Saturdays had been made obligatory by Act of Parliament. All of a sudden the working man and his family were able to enjoy days out, take holidays, and see a little more of the world.

With typical business acumen, Francis Frith foresaw that these new tourists would enjoy having souvenirs to commemorate their days out. For the next thirty years he travelled the country by train and by pony and trap, producing fine photographs of seaside resorts and beauty spots that were keenly bought by millions of Victorians. These prints were painstakingly pasted into family albums and pored over during the dark nights of winter, rekindling precious memories of summer excursions. Frith's studio was soon supplying retail shops all over the country, and by 1890 F Frith & Co had become the greatest specialist photographic publishing company in the world, with over 2,000 sales outlets, and pioneered the picture postcard.

## FRANCIS FRITH'S LEGACY

Francis Frith had died in 1898 at his villa in Cannes, his great project still growing. By 1970 the archive he created contained over a third of a million pictures showing 7,000 British towns and villages.

Frith's legacy to us today is of immense significance and value, for the magnificent archive of evocative photographs he created provides a unique record of change in the cities, towns and villages throughout Britain over a century and more. Frith and his fellow studio photographers revisited locations many times down the years to update their views, compiling for us an enthralling and colourful pageant of British life and character.

We are fortunate that Frith was dedicated to recording the minutiae of everyday life. For it is this sheer wealth of visual data, the painstaking chronicle of changes in dress, transport, street layouts, buildings, housing and landscape that captivates us so much today, offering us a powerful link with the past and with the lives of our ancestors.

Computers have now made it possible for Frith's many thousands of images to be accessed almost instantly. The archive offers every one of us an opportunity to examine the places where we and our families have lived and worked down the years. Its images, depicting our shared past, are now bringing pleasure and enlightenment to millions around the world a century and more after his death.

For further information visit: www.francisfrith.com

## INTERIOR DECORATION

Frith's photographs can be seen framed and as giant wall murals in thousands of pubs, restaurants, hotels, banks, retail stores and other public buildings throughout Britain. These provide interesting and attractive décor, generating strong local interest and acting as a powerful reminder of gentler days in our increasingly busy and frenetic world.

## FRITH PRODUCTS

All Frith photographs are available as prints and posters in a variety of different sizes and styles. In the UK we also offer a range of other gift and stationery products illustrated with Frith photographs, although many of these are not available for delivery outside the UK – see our web site for more information on the products available for delivery in your country.

## THE INTERNET

Over 100,000 photographs of Britain can be viewed and purchased on the Frith web site. The web site also includes memories and reminiscences contributed by our customers, who have personal knowledge of localities and of the people and properties depicted in Frith photographs. If you wish to learn more about a specific town or village you may find these reminiscences fascinating to browse. Why not add your own comments if you think they would be of interest to others? See **www.francisfrith.com**

## PLEASE HELP US BRING FRITH'S PHOTOGRAPHS TO LIFE

Our authors do their best to recount the history of the places they write about. They give insights into how particular towns and villages developed, they describe the architecture of streets and buildings, and they discuss the lives of famous people who lived there. But however knowledgeable our authors are, the story they tell is necessarily incomplete.

Frith's photographs are so much more than plain historical documents. They are living proofs of the flow of human life down the generations. They show real people at real moments in history; and each of those people is the son or daughter of someone, the brother or sister, aunt or uncle, grandfather or grandmother of someone else. All of them lived, worked and played in the streets depicted in Frith's photographs.

We would be grateful if you would give us your insights into the places shown in our photographs: the streets and buildings, the shops, businesses and industries. Post your memories of life in those streets on the Frith website: what it was like growing up there, who ran the local shop and what shopping was like years ago; if your workplace is shown tell us about your working day and what the building is used for now. Read other visitors' memories and reconnect with your shared local history and heritage. With your help more and more Frith photographs can be brought to life, and vital memories preserved for posterity, and for the benefit of historians in the future.

Wherever possible, we will try to include some of your comments in future editions of our books. Moreover, if you spot errors in dates, titles or other facts, please let us know, because our archive records are not always completely accurate—they rely on 140 years of human endeavour and hand-compiled records. You can email us using the contact form on the website.

Thank you!

For further information, trade, or author enquiries
please contact us at the address below:

**The Francis Frith Collection, 6 Oakley Business Park,
Wylye Road, Dinton, Wiltshire SP3 5EU.**
Tel: +44 (0)1722 716 376  Fax: +44 (0)1722 716 881
e-mail: sales@francisfrith.co.uk  **www.francisfrith.com**